The Book of Think

(Or How to Solve a Problem Twice Your Size)

Written by MARILYN BURNS

Illustrated by MARTHA WESTON

LITTLE, BROWN AND COMPANY
Boston   New York
Toronto   London

This Brown Paper School book was edited and prepared for publication at The Yolla Bolly Press, Covelo, California, between November 1975 and May 1976. The series is under the supervision of James and Carolyn Robertson. Production staff members are: Colleen Carter, Sharon Miley, and Gene Floyd.

Published simultaneously in Canada by
Little, Brown & Company (Canada) Limited.
Printed in the United States of America.

HC: 10   BP

PB: 20   19   BB

Library of Congress Cataloging in Publication Data

Burns, Marilyn.
    The book of think.

    (The brown paper school)
    1. Problem solving. 2. Problem solving — Problems, exercises, etc.
I. Title.
BF441.B93   153.4'3   76-17848
ISBN 0-316-11742-0
ISBN 0-316-11743-9 pbk.

This book is for anyone
who has at least one problem.

What's in This Book

Thinking Hard Doesn't Always Work

What would you do if you lost your money on the way to the movies? Or you were eating at a friend's house and there was something real weird and funny-smelling on your plate? Suppose you found out that your best friend was stealing from your uncle's store. What if you took the wrong bus or subway and wound up in a part of town that didn't feel friendly?

Running into problems in your life is a sure thing. As sure as having to brush your teeth. You've got what you need to solve problems — your brain. Along with lots of past practice in using it.

What's important is not just using your brain, but *how* you use it. Sometimes thinking hard seems like the only way to solve a problem. But that doesn't always work. If you're not thinking in the right way, it's very easy to get stuck.

Sometimes people say things like this: *It can't be solved. I don't know how. I give up.* That will never do. There is always another way to look at a problem. That's what this book is about: looking at problems and learning to think in new ways.

There's more than one way to think.

Part One:

Getting Out of Your
Own Way

Sometimes you get in the way of your own brain. Your thinking gets stuck. Sometimes you build your own mental walls. Then you keep bumping into them.

These are problems everyone has.

In this book, you'll learn about why you do get in your own way. There are examples to help you understand how to avoid this. And there are exercises to help you warm up your brain. To get it going in helpful directions.

Read on. Try the warm-ups. You'll be amazed how you can get out of your own way.

Tackling What You Know Best — You

Mental wall number one: not seeing what's under your very nose.

Without looking, what color socks are you wearing? Look and check.

When you fold your arms (no, don't do it yet), one hand is on top, one is tucked in. Do you know which is which for you? Guess first. Then try it.

When you're getting dressed in the morning, which sock do you put on first? Check and see tomorrow.

How about when you clasp your hands? Which thumb is on top?

Are you right-handed or left-handed? That you know for sure. But did you know if you were right-thumbed or left-thumbed before you tried it? Clasping your hands is something you do automatically when you need to. You don't give it a second thought. But there was a time when you had to learn how to do that. Then you gave it lots of attention. Now you give it no attention. Try to clasp your hands the other way. How does it feel?

If you had an empty paper tube to look through, which eye would you use?

There are lots of things about yourself that you've been living with for a long time without noticing.

That must stop!

The first step in becoming a successful problem solver is not to let your own nose get in your way.

What else don't you ever bother to see about yourself?

Looking at What You Usually See

What else has your brain been ignoring lately?

Think of the telephone dial. (Don't look at one yet.) Imagine which letters go where. There are ten holes. There are twenty-six letters in the alphabet. You've seen that dial lots of times. Okay, which letters of the alphabet aren't on the dial? (Long division isn't much help, either.) Make a sketch of the dial. Put in the numbers, too. Then check it.

There just isn't room inside your head to store all the information you get. You might think of your brain as a sponge. It will only hold so much. Enough is enough. Besides, you don't really need to remember where the numbers and letters are on the telephone dial. They're in the right place when you need them.

Keeping details in your head isn't always a good idea. Learning to look is. Noticing is good exercise: it helps you see things you've been ignoring all this time.

Try this quiz. Answer true or false. See how you score.

1. The Statue of Liberty uses her right hand to hold the torch.
2. A record on a record player turns in a clockwise direction.
3. Lincoln's head on a penny faces left.
4. Your bedroom door opens in toward your bedroom.
5. The buttonholes on a man's shirt point up and down.
6. Page fifty-two of this book is a right-hand page.
7. The jack of spades is a one-eyed jack.
8. The stripes on a zebra's legs are horizontal.
9. The person who illustrated this book is a woman.
10. Most pencils have eight sides.

Which were you absolutely sure about? Which did you have
to guess? Wait a few days or a week and try the quiz again.
See which information you kept stored in your head.

Imagine you are in your kitchen. What's usually on the kitchen table? On the counter next to the sink? Think of all the things you can. Then go and see how much your mind's eye has remembered.

Here are some things to check in school tomorrow. Think of the kids in your class. Who is left-handed? Make a list and then test it.

What about people who wear glasses? List the kids in your class first. Then think of the grown-ups at school: the principal, the school secretary, the librarian, the teachers. Can you list ten people who wear glasses? Twenty? Check it.

Keep looking at ordinary things. Look at them as if you're seeing them for the first time. You'll see lots of new things you've never looked at before.

Tunnel Vision

Most likely you don't have tunnel vision. You can test yourself easily.

Hold a finger up in front of you. Look straight ahead, kind of like looking through your finger. Keep looking straight ahead. Don't move your eyes, but slowly move your finger around toward your ear. Wiggling your finger as you move it helps.

Even though you're looking straight ahead, you should be able to see your finger. That's because you can see out of the corner of your eye. That space where you can see things even though you're not looking there is called your periphery. (Even if you can't say it, you've still got it.)

When horses were used in cities for pulling wagons, they often wore blinders. The blinders were like walls, shutting off the periphery. Horses wore them so they wouldn't get frightened or distracted and upset the applecart. Make your own blinders with your hands, so you can cut off your own periphery.

Back to the brain. Watch out for mental blinders. They'll get in the way of the problem solver every time. They often stop you from seeing out of the corner of your brain and solving the problem.

Here's an old problem that shows this.

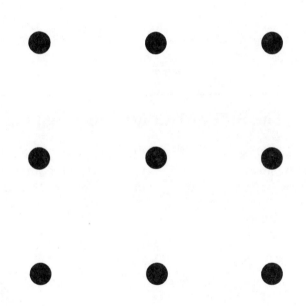

Draw nine dots like this on a piece of paper. Now, without lifting your pencil, draw through all of the nine dots using only four straight lines.

(Hint: Don't box yourself in.)

To solve the nine dot problem, you can't let mental blinders keep you inside the square of the nine dots. You need to let your mind outside the corners. Like this:

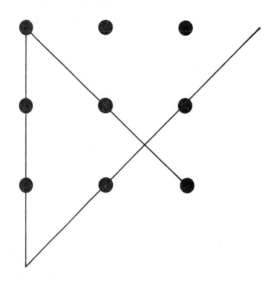

The Story of Columbus's Egg

Christopher Columbus did not have a problem with mental blinders. When he returned from his voyage of great discoveries, there was a royal banquet in his honor. Some of the members of the court who hadn't been on the trip seemed unimpressed.

"Big deal," they said. "Anyone sailing out in that direction would have bumped into the New World. That was no problem."

Columbus answered by suggesting a problem right there. He chose one of the eggs from a plate on the table. They were hard-cooked, but unshelled. "Can you make this egg stand on its end?"

The hecklers tried. And tried. "This is different," they said. "This can't be done."

"But look," said Columbus. He smashed the egg against the table, crushing the tip of the shell. The egg stood on its own.

Moral: Once a problem is solved, the solution seems so obvious. Finding the answer is sometimes a case of not making your brain just stare straight ahead.

Don't forget your periphery. (Can you say it yet?)

SHARPENING YOUR SENSES

An important part of brain exercising is using all of your senses. Most people don't. It's another example of not using what you have. Problem solvers need all the help they can find.

Try to imagine the things listed below. You can rate yourself on each one: easy, hard, can't do it at all.

Imagine the taste of peanuts.
Imagine the smell of gasoline.
Imagine the sound of a car starting.
Imagine the feel of swinging high on a swing.
Imagine the taste of a banana.
Imagine the smell of toothpaste.
Imagine the sound of a dropped book hitting the floor.
Imagine the feel of biting into an apple.

Why is this important at all? Remember, someone invented pizza. And someone first got the idea for soft drinks. There wasn't always real soft fabric for pajamas. You can bet who-ever invented these things did more than just look.

Who knows when there will be a terrible shortage of meat? You might be asked to invent the perfect substitute for the hamburger. It had better taste good, smell good, and be a good chew.

On with more complicated "imagine" exercises.

Imagine the taste of chocolate ice cream changing into the
  taste of a piece of orange.
Imagine the feel of hopping on one foot changing into the
  feel of skipping.
Imagine the smell of bread toasting changing into the smell
  of peanut butter.
Imagine the sound of a friend laughing changing into the
  sound of a baseball bat hitting the ball.

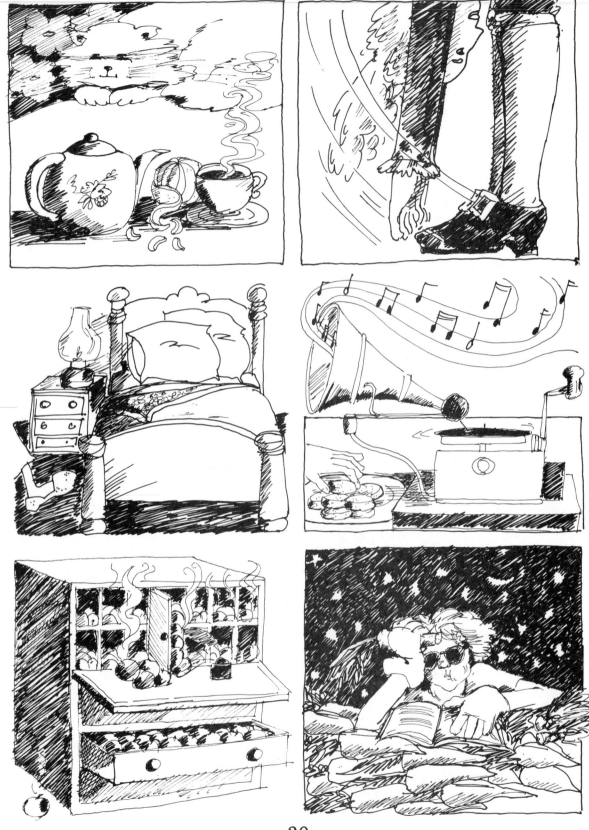

When people need to concentrate on something special they sometimes close their eyes. Or stare off into space. That's because too much is feeding the brain at one time. It's called sensory overload. Cutting down on what you see leaves more room in your brain.

Ever hear your Mom call, "Shut that radio off!" — one of those times when she really means it? It may be that she has a case of sensory overload.

Different people have different sensory needs when they think. Your own needs are important for you to explore. Do you need absolute silence? A sunny day? Warm socks on your feet?

Some people have had interesting specific needs.

Dr. Samuel Johnson had to have a purring cat, orange peel, and tea.
Mozart needed to exercise.
Immanuel Kant liked to work in bed at times, with the blankets arranged around him in his own special way.
Hart Crane played jazz loudly on a Victrola.
Johann Schiller needed to fill his desk with rotten apples.

Let's move on from imagining to the real thing. All of our senses are linked. Here are some ways to learn more about that. In each of these exercises, you'll be using just one sense.

You'll need a friend for these. That way you can help each other sharpen your senses. The world can't have too many good problem solvers.

Exercise No. 1: Just Tasting

You need some bite-size pieces of food that are all crunchy in the same way. Like apple, carrot, onion, raw potato, turnip. One of you needs to close your eyes and hold your nose. The other should put a piece of one of the foods in your mouth. Guess what it is. Try this for several different foods, and then switch so the other person can explore their tasting sense.

Try it with creamy things too — ice cream, peanut butter, pudding, sour cream, leftover mashed potatoes.

And then use things that you drink. Milk, orange juice, water, whatever. Try different flavors of chewing gum.

Is your taste linked more to your sight or smell? Can you feel the differences between things with only your sense of taste?

Exercise No. 2: Guess What?

This exercise is for your sense of hearing. One of you closes your eyes. The other makes some sound, using whatever is handy in the room. One idea is tapping a pencil on the table or on the floor. Try ruffling the pages of a book. Or unscrewing the lid of a jar. Take turns. Each one try to stump the other.

Can your sense of hearing improve? Were the same kinds of sounds difficult for each of you?

Exercise No. 3: The Walnut Game

An extra friend or two makes this a trickier exercise. You need some unopened walnuts, one for each person and one extra. You also need a small paper sack to hold them. Each person draws a walnut out of the sack. Leave the extra in there. It is the group walnut.

The rules are: Do not look at your walnut. Feel it with your hands. Explore it until you think you could put it back in the sack with the others and be able to pick it out.

After each of you is satisfied that you "know" your walnut, put them back in the sack. But first remove the group walnut. Pass it around until each person is sure they could identify that one too. Then put it back in the sack.

Now everyone tries to find their own walnut and identify the group walnut. Pass them around until everyone is satisfied. Looking now is okay. Does it help?

Wandering Outside

More exercises for observing the ordinary. Outside this time.
But first, find some comfortable place at home so you can
wander just with your head.

Here are three possible exercises. They're all geared to giving
you another look at what you usually see. Read them
through. Then pick one to try on your first real trip out.

Exercise No. 1: Taking In the Usual

These are questions about things you might see on any walk
or bike ride. Try to answer them first. Then check as many
as you can out in the world.

On traffic lights, which color is on top?
Does a stop sign have six sides or eight?
Is there a street sign at every corner of an intersection?
If not, how many are there, usually?
Do the numbers on the houses on your street go by two's, or
four's, or what?
Is there a public telephone near your house?
On which side of it is the coin return slot?
Are there telephone poles on your block? How many?

Exercise No. 2: A Color Walk

Imagine a walk you've taken lots of times. Like to school, or to a friend's house, or to the store.

Now, choose a color. Make a list of all the things you usually see on that walk which are the color you've chosen. Then check out your list.

Exercise No. 3: A Friendly Block

This one is good to do with a friend. Think of a block you both walk down often. A block you both feel familiar with. Each of you makes your own list of all the stores and buildings on that block. Include trees too, and telephone poles, and whatever else you can think of. Exchange lists. Then take the walk and check each other.

Did you both list the same things?

The trick is — don't ignore what's out there. Okay, out the
front door. (Did it open in or out?)

What's Right Here?

You need practice stretching your brain. Looking at things in other ways.

Like this. What's the message?

Did you see it right away? Does it help if the page is closer or farther away? Ask others to try it. Find out what people usually see first.

Sometimes the problem isn't even looking at something a new way. Sometimes the problem is that you see what you expect to see. Not good. It's important to look carefully.

Try these:

Sometimes your mind is
is quicker than your eye.

What do you think might be the
the funny thing about this saying?

Do you usually make the
the same mistake twice?

Sometimes there just isn't enough information to be sure what you think. Still, it's important not to get stuck. To look at it as many ways as possible.

Here is part of a picture. The entire picture appears on the next page. Before you turn the page and look, try to figure out what it is. Don't stop at your first thought. Keep going until you run out. Or until you just can't wait one more second to turn the page.

After you've done it, ask someone else to try. Did they guess different things? Try to understand what it is they saw.

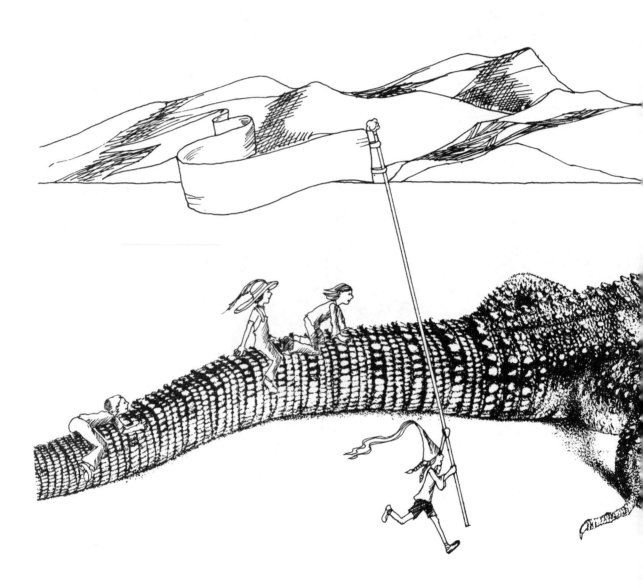

Crazy Connections

Problem solving can be serious stuff.

Don't fool around.
Get down to business.
Don't play around.
Don't be lazy.
Think.

All that may be. But if you only look at thinking as serious business, then you're missing an important key. Sometimes letting your mind play is a good idea. Even being silly.

Good jokes and riddles are funny. Some clever thinkers had to think of them. Do you think they sat down seriously to write one hundred clever jokes and riddles?

The punch lines of jokes and riddles are often totally unexpected. That's one reason why some make us laugh. They connect things you never thought of as connectables.

Joke No. 1

A man was sitting on a park bench. He had a banana in his ear. A girl was skipping by. She stopped. "Excuse me," she said, "you have a banana in your ear." "What?" the man answered. "I said, you've got a banana in your ear," she told him again. "What's that?" he said. "Mister," she said, getting exasperated, "you've got a banana sticking out of your ear." "I'm sorry," he answered, "I can't hear you. I've got a banana in my ear."

43

Joke No. 2

A student eating lunch in the school cafeteria was piling his dessert of coffee ice cream on his head. The ice cream was dripping through his hair. Finally the teacher on duty noticed and raced over. "What's going on here? How come you're piling the coffee ice cream on your head?" The boy answered, "Uh oh, is it coffee? I thought it was chocolate."

Two examples of the same thing. Something unexpected. Here's an exercise to help you connect the unconnectable. It's called Think a Link.

The words in the groups below don't seem to have much to do with each other. Try to think of a link. Something they have in common. Try to link them in more than one way.

pencil	apple	football
flower	lamp	lemon
basket	stapler	clay
tree	telephone	clock

Try these with a friend, or around the dinner table. Compare your connects. There are no right answers. But this kind of thinking can come in handy when you are faced with a problem. Any connect could be the leading clue. And once in a while, you get a funny riddle from the bunch.

There are two sides to your brain. You can think of yourself as having two minds. The left-hand side of your brain controls the kind of thinking that is logical, orderly. Like solving a step-by-step math problem. That side also takes charge of your speech and hearing. The right-hand side of your brain rules over a different kind of thinking. Not-so-logical things like feelings, experiences, inventions, appreciation of art and music. To decide that one kind of thinking is better than the other is another example of getting in your own way. Both sides are equally important. They each help you make different connections. Being mentally lopsided is no way to become a successful problem solver.

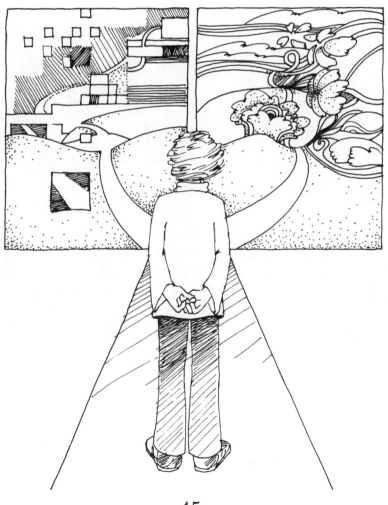

Do You Know the People You Know?

There are times when it's nice not to be all alone with a problem. That's when friends can help. It's not always easy to ask. It's not always easy to know who to ask.

Have you thought about which of your friends are helpful problem solvers? Would you go to all of them with the same kinds of problems?

There are some friends who always agree with everything you say. That may be because they like you a lot. They want you to feel better. They might even tell you not to worry, that the problem will go away soon. Is that always the best help?

Some people always have the solution. They tell you right away what they would do. See, it's easy, they say. Maybe their solution works for you. Maybe not. Have they helped you think about yourself?

Some people like to laugh a lot. That's super. Except sometimes. Like in the middle of a mouthful of mashed potatoes. Or when you come to them with a problem. A real problem.

There are people who love to talk. You ask about a problem. They begin to talk. And talk. And talk. And somehow you can't quite remember what the problem was. Which may be fine . . . until tomorrow morning.

Think about the kind of help you would like to get when you go to someone with a problem. Then think about the people you know. Who do you think would be able to help you? In a way that would really help.

Want to find out? Here's an exercise for you to try.

You need an idea. Maybe a new one. Maybe an idea you've had for a while. An invention. A new board game that you think is fun to play. That could be as popular as checkers. A story or poem you wrote that you really like. A neat way to build a loft in your room if you could only convince your parents.

Then tell your idea to different friends at different times. Tell it seriously. You might even tell it to someone you don't think of as a friend. (You might change your mind about that person.)

Note how people react. Are they polite? Willing to listen? Interested in helping?

Now, how people react may tell you something about your idea. If you suggest the invention of a fur-lined coffee cup to keep coffee hot longer, your friends may laugh. Or look at you funny. Maybe they ought to.

You may want to try out what you think is a good idea and then a crummy one on the same people.

The idea is to learn more about people you know.

The Dictionary Game

Here's another way to look at people you know. It's a game that will help you learn more about how others think.

You need at least four people to play. You'll also need: Some paper (a small pad of note paper is good). A pencil for each player. And a dictionary.

The rules: One person looks in the dictionary for a word that no one knows. There are plenty to choose from.

Then each person invents a possible definition of that word and writes it down. The person with the dictionary writes the real definition. Even if there are several definitions in the dictionary, one is enough. Or it may be shortened if it's really long.

All the definitions go to the dictionary person. That person now reads all the definitions. Including the real one. Each player then has to try to guess the right definition.

Suppose the word is 'bailey'. Which of these is the right definition?

A stringed instrument used in Yugoslavia.
The court of a medieval castle.
A dance popular in England in the nineteenth century.
An insect which attacks tropical plants.

Choose one. Then check the dictionary.

Keep score like this: A person scores one point if they guess the right definition. A person scores one point every time someone chooses their definition.

You can change the dictionary person each time. Or every three times. Or however. That's up to those playing the game.

Here's what you should look for: Who are the shrewd guessers? Who seems to write definitions that get chosen a lot? Who goofs off and doesn't even care?

What new can you learn about people? What can you do with this information?

There Are at Least Two Ways
to Look at Something

It's easy to look at something. You see what you see. And that's the end of that.

But watch out.

That's you stopping you from exploring other possibilities. Getting in your own way again.

A mirror reverses your image from left to right. Have you ever wondered why it doesn't reverse it top to bottom also? Have you ever wondered why you never wondered about that?

Optical illusions play tricks on your brain. They say, "Hey, look again. Something else is happening here." Then you look more carefully to see what it is.

There are some optical illusions that look absolutely possible. But they aren't. No matter how you look at them.

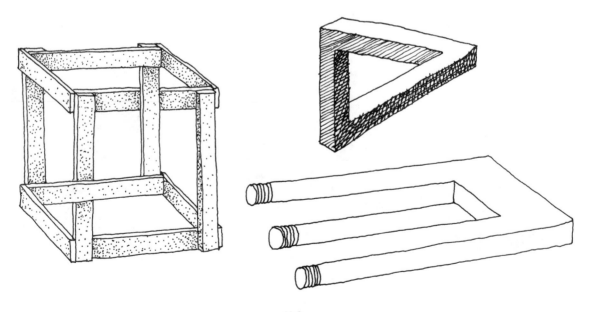

Some look like something they aren't. You can prove it to yourself.

Are the curved lines curved?

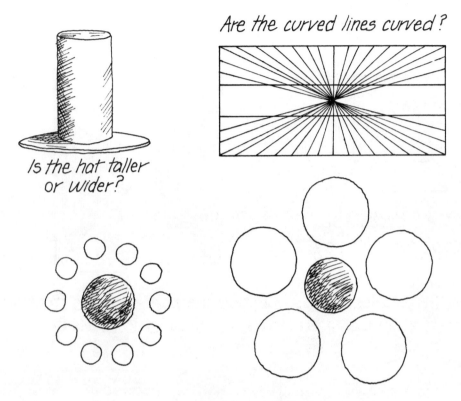

Is the hat taller or wider?

Which shaded circle seems bigger? Is it?

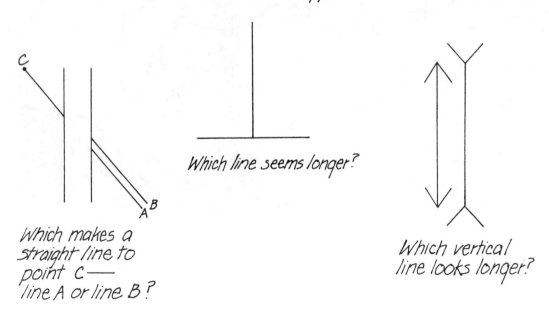

Which makes a straight line to point C — line A or line B?

Which line seems longer?

Which vertical line looks longer?

Some illusions can be looked at two different ways. Look at each for a bit. You will switch back and forth from seeing one thing to another.

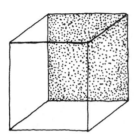

Is the shaded side inside or outside?

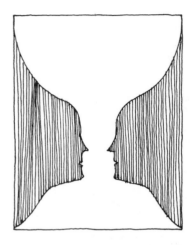

Do you see the profiles first or the goblet?

Which is easier for you to see — the rabbit or the duck?

Can you find both the old woman and the young woman?

The next step: Getting your brain to serve you that way when there's no optical puzzle. One way to practice is by purposely thinking about the same thing in more than one way.

Like this: Picture a glass half filled with water. Is the glass half-full? Or half-empty?

Try these.

Do the walls of a house hold up the roof? Or does the roof keep the walls from falling in? Or falling out?

Is the girl picking up the box? Or putting it down?

Is the boy jumping up? Or coming down?

Is the girl walking toward the tree? Or away from the house?

Putting Your Foot In Your Brain

Have you ever put your foot in your mouth? Not really. That means you said something and right away you wished you hadn't said it. It's not so easy to get your foot out of your mouth. Once it's said, it's said.

Usually that happens because your mouth got going before your brain did. Putting your foot in your brain is kind of like that. It's another one of those mental pitfalls to watch out for. It has to do with deciding something too soon. Mostly when you haven't really looked at all the possibilities. And then your mind is made up. It's another way to get stuck.

Try this problem:

The Dentist Problem

A boy went to the dentist to get a cavity filled. The boy was the dentist's son, but the dentist was not the boy's father. How can this be?

No tricks. The boy really was the son of the dentist. The dentist really was the boy's parent. The dentist was his mother.

What makes this tricky? There are more men who are dentists than women. So it's easy to picture a man when you imagine a dentist.

That's an example of having a preconceived idea. You brought some information with you to the problem. It was stored up there in your brain. If you weren't able to solve the problem, it may be that your information was your own mental wall.

Here's a second chance. Try to keep your foot out of your brain this time.

The Doctor Problem

Sally was riding her bike near her house when she was hit by a truck. Her father was there, and raced her to the emergency room at the hospital. They wheeled her into the operating room. "Oh, no," the surgeon cried. "I can't operate on this child. She's my daughter!" What's happening here?

Same story, really. Just some different information. And it is so obvious — when you know the answer.

Where do your preconceived ideas come from? That's something to think about. The more you understand about your preconceived ideas, the easier it is to avoid pitfalls.

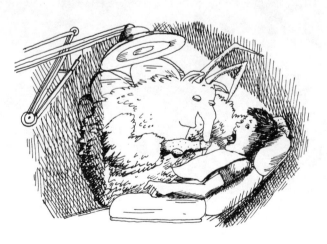

Here's an "imagine" quiz: Suppose you moved. You went to the new school on Friday to register. Monday was to be your first day. You were given this picture of some of the kids in your new class. You haven't met any of them yet.

Take special note of your first impressions. Ask yourself these questions:

Who in the picture would you like for a friend?
Who would be good to ask for help on a hard assignment?
Who do you think is the best athlete?
Who looks most like you?
Did you choose that kid for any of your answers?

Now what does this tell you about yourself? How you answered the questions about the picture may have given you some ideas. But, you may have some stereotypes.

Stereotypes come from preconceived ideas. We use clues to come to conclusions. And often use the same clues over and over.

Sometimes that's helpful. Suppose you're in the supermarket. You can't find the smoked oysters your father asked you to buy. It's a good idea to ask the person wearing that smock-type uniform. The uniform gives you a clue: that person probably works here.

But sometimes stereotyping can lead you smack into a mental wall. Like thinking a dentist must be a man. Or that kid with glasses on in the picture couldn't possibly be a good athlete.

Sizing Up Shoes

Here's an exercise to help you learn about how you stereotype people. It's especially easy to do on buses, or anyplace where you can look at people without being rude.

What you do is to look at someone's shoes before looking at their face. Now, imagine what that person will look like. Male or female? Young or old? What kind of clothes are they wearing?

Then check your guesses.

Try it from top to bottom too. Can faces tell you about shoes?

If someone says, "Hey, kid, have you got some kind of problem?" take a deep breath. And explain that you're exploring your own stereotypes and preconceived ideas. That you're learning how to break down mental walls.

Then keep sizing up.

Part Two:

Knowing a Problem When You See It

How do you get a problem?

There isn't just one answer to that question. Problems come in different ways. And there's no telling when one will appear.

But there is a moment when you first realize that there is a problem. You know for sure, because you've got it.

Problems All Start Somewhere

It's not always enough to know you've got a problem. Sometimes it helps to see where it came from. That's not always easy: problems creep up in different ways.

First way: You notice something isn't quite right. Not the way it should be. Like hamburgers for supper are your favorite. But the ones you just got look like someone stepped on them before they got to your plate. Or you did a long division problem for homework. And the remainder you got was bigger than what you started with.

Another way: Someone brings a problem right to you. Your brother tells you at nine o'clock at night that he hasn't started his report for school. It's due tomorrow, and he needs your help.

A third way: Maybe something has been bothering you for a while. You finally decide that it isn't going away, so you'd better do something about it. It could be you misplaced that one piece of a game. It's just not the same using a piece of paper because it always blows off the board. Or here comes the bus and once again you don't have the exact change you need.

One more way: You do something and all of a sudden you're in the middle of a problem. Like you stopped on the way home from school to make sure a little kid who was crying wasn't hurt. You put down the books you were carrying. When you left, you forgot to pick them up. And now it's midnight, and it's raining.

Can you think of other ways problems can appear? Can you think of other ways you've first noticed them?

What's the Real Problem?

Okay, you know there is a problem. Now that you've got it, are you sure what it is?

Take the yukky hamburgers. Is the problem that there is no way you can possibly eat them? Or that there is something wrong with the person that cooked them? Or that now you need to find a new family to live with?

About the problem of the exact change bus. Is the problem how are you going to get the exact change before the bus comes? Or what can you do after you get on the bus without it? Or how can you get to school another way? Maybe the thing to do is to go right back to the house and back to bed. Would that solve the problem?

Suppose you come home and no one is there. And you can't find your key. What you do about it depends on what you think is the problem. Here are some possible ways to state the problem:

How can you get the door open without a key?
How else can you get into the house?
What could you do while waiting for someone else to come home?
How can you get another key because your mother said she'd kill you if you lost one more?

Which do you think is the problem? Or do you think the problem is something else?

It isn't always easy to decide what the problem is. But that's the important first step. No use solving the wrong problem. You probably won't be able to save that solution for anything.

What Problems Did Mother Goose Have?

Some problem exercises for you to try. There aren't any right answers to these questions. There are several possibilities for each, so they're good practice.

Mother Goose managed to give some of her characters some problems. Try and figure who's got the problem, and what it is.

Remember the old woman who lived in a shoe with all those children? When she didn't know what to do, she gave them broth without bread, whipped them, and sent them to bed.

The old woman seemed to have a problem. Maybe tunnel vision. Maybe sensory overload from her children. The children had a problem too. Who's got the biggest problem? What is it?

How about Georgie Porgy? He had the habit of kissing the girls. That made them cry. And then when the boys came out, he ran away.

The girls had a problem there. But George sure doesn't seem quite right. What is the problem? What could be done about it?

Peter Piper spent a lot of time picking pickled peppers. What about this peck of pickled peppers that Peter Piper picked?

Peter's got a problem. But maybe you have the bigger problem here. Can you say that rhyme without goofing?

The important thing is this: when there is something to be
solved, look at it carefully. What is it that needs to be
solved? Be careful when you choose the problem to work on.

Who was Mother Goose anyway?

Part Three:

Brain Push-Ups

Getting out of the way of your brain was the first step. Then came knowing a problem when you've got it. What comes next?

In this section, you'll learn different ways to tackle problems. Also, you'll get plenty of problems and exercises for practice.

Don't just read. Do the push-ups. Try to figure out the problems for yourself. That feels best. Next best is when you figure them out with a bit of a hint. It's even okay to peek at the answer when you just have to know.

But most important is this: Look at how you think, and how you get stuck. When you've got a solution, try to figure how it can help you next time.

Don't Fall for What Pops In First

An exercise problem: Get a dollar bill and a quarter. Now, balance the quarter on the edge of the dollar bill. No props allowed.

Your first reaction is important. Imagine the quarter balancing on the edge of the bill. What do you see in your head? Could it really balance like that? With no hands?

If not, get that right out of your head! Take charge. Don't fall for your own first thought. Stand up to your brain.

Look, there's got to be another way. A quarter can't sit on that skinny edge. You've either got to do something with that quarter. Or with that edge.

(Hint: There is something you could do to that edge. A quarter really can sit on it. And comfortably too.)

If you've been reading along without a dollar bill and a quarter, you've cut down on your chances of solving this. Give your head a hand.

Here are two possible solutions:

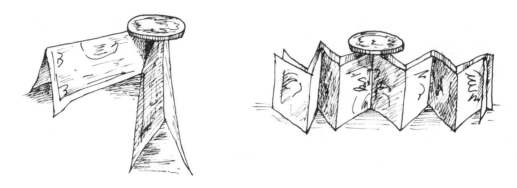

Throwing out what pops in first is a useful way to attack some problems. It keeps you from stumbling into two mental holes. One is tunnel vision. (Remember the blinders?) The other is looking at something only one way.

Here is more exercise, while you've got that dollar bill and the quarter handy:

Get two glasses or tin cans that are the same height. Place them so your fist can fit in between. The dollar bill should reach across them.

The problem: The quarter needs to stand in the middle of the dollar bill which is stretched across the two glasses or cans.

Try it. No, the quarter can't rest on either glass. No, you can't move the glasses closer. Now, throw out what you just tried and look at it another way. The dollar bill isn't strong enough to stretch across and hold the quarter. What can you do about that?

Here are some push-ups. They seem different, but they all have one thing in common: what first pops into your head may be no use at all. You've got to do something else with what you're given. Put out those first thoughts. Look another way.

Toothpicking Triangles

You can make a triangle that has three sides the same length with three toothpicks. If you had six toothpicks, you could make two triangles. Actually, you could make two triangles with equal sides with only five toothpicks.

Here's the problem: Use six toothpicks and make four triangles that all have the same length sides.

Blowing Bits

There are five bits of paper in the palm of your hand. You need to blow them off. But one by one. How can you do this?

Face to Face

You need one sheet from a newspaper. How can two people stand on the same sheet, face to face, so they can't possibly touch each other? No, the people's hands aren't tied. And you can't tear the sheet of newspaper.

Puzzling Ping-Pong

There's a Ping-Pong ball in a hole. The hole is just a little bit bigger around than the ball. It's longer than your arm is. Or anyone else's arm. There are no long sticks around. What can you do to get the ball out of the hole?

Practice ignoring what pops into your head first. Sometimes you may throw out an idea that was pretty good. But it wasn't getting you anywhere. Besides, there's always another way to look at something. That's the key. Looking at what's there in a different way.

List Before You Look

Making lists is another way to take on problems. Mostly people make lists to help them remember things. Like shopping lists. Or chores. Or homework assignments. Things that have to get done.

Another use for lists is to help you think. In two ways. By looking at things in different ways. By looking at things in more ways.

Here are some list-making warm-ups. You can do these exercises alone or with a friend. Comparing lists is fun. (Don't use skimpy pieces of scratch paper. Give yourself some space to list.)

Things You Know

These are things you need to pull out of your memory. The idea is to list lots. No time limit. Stop when you've thought of all you can.

List all the foods you can think of that are yellow.
List all the games you know for two people to play.
List all the things that bug you.
List all the ice cream flavors you can think of.

There are some things you should notice while you're listing. How did you get started? After you've listed all the easy ones, what did you do? How did you decide when to give up?

Things That Could Be

These lists are not of things you know. They are of things you could do with what you know. This time, set a time limit for each list. Two minutes.

List all the uses that could be made of an empty tin can.
List all the ways you could make a skateboard go uphill by itself.
List ways that a kid could earn money.
List all the things you could do to improve where you live.

How did this kind of list compare with the first warm-up? Did the time limit make a difference? Which lists were longer? Which were more fun to do?

What's Going On Here?

List all the possible things that could be happening here. Watch out for your preconceived ideas. Try this with pictures in books, magazines, newspapers.

On to practice problems. Here are three more chances to make lists. Then try out the ideas you listed.

Practice Problem No. 1:

How many ways can you turn a glass of water upside down without spilling the water? Here are some possibilities to get you started:

Freeze it.
Lower it into a sink full of water and turn it upside down below the surface.
Hold it at arm's length and swing it over your head. Outside, please.

Keep listing.

Practice Problem No. 2:

How many ways can you empty a glass of water which is sitting on a table without touching either the glass or the table?

Practice Problem No. 3:

How can you design a glass that won't spill?

The answer to the dollar bill, the quarter and the two glasses problem: Fold the dollar bill like an accordion. Then it will hold the quarter.

Making lists in these exercises is one thing. Using them to solve real problems in your life is another. That takes some effort.

Start by making a list of all the problems you have. Which ones haven't you thought of for a while? Which aren't really problems at all?

Do any of them happen over and over? Like having a hassle with the same person? Then take that one and list all the ways that problem gets started. If the problem keeps coming back, then there's something you haven't been doing right.

Remember that trap of looking at something only one way. Try listing before you look.

Logic Isn't the Only Way

Be logical. That's a method you've heard about for solving problems.

Here's what you do when you use logic. You pick a direction for your thinking to go in. Then you go step-by-step. You check that each step along the way makes sense. And hopefully you get to what you were looking for.

The big catch: Which direction should you go in? Somehow you need a mental push. If you get a push in the wrong direction, logic takes you to the wrong place. If you don't get a push in any direction, logic won't take you anywhere.

A candy bar can last forever with logic. All you have to do is not to eat it all at once. Just eat half. Then put it away. Next time you take a nibble, eat just half of what's there. Then put it away again. Keep eating half of what you've got each time. You can't ever eat it all that way.

Logically, that is.

Using logic can make you richer. Maybe.

The reasoning is logical. Somehow, it just isn't reasonable.

Learning to solve problems doesn't mean learning to be more logical. It means learning to think in different ways. Not always in a straight line.

Logic can be the perfect way to reason up to a problem. When it works, it's terrific. When it doesn't, being logical is as little help as thinking hard.

Starting at the End

Sometimes you know where you need to end up. But, it's the getting there that's the problem.

There may be more than one way to find a solution. It sure would be nice to find at least one way. It would be super to find the best way.

Going backwards is sometimes a better way to go. It can save you time. It can make the problem a lot easier.

Like here. Which person caught the fish?

Tracing from a pole could give you the solution in one step. But it could take three. Following the line from the fish up gives you better odds for a quicker solution.

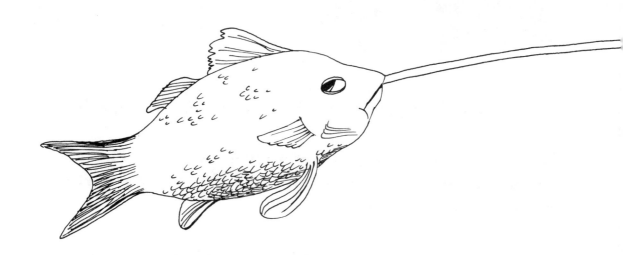

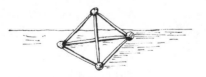

The answer to "Toothpicking Triangles": It can be done like this with clay. What made you think the toothpicks had to lie flat on the table?

The Ten Pennies Problem

Here's a problem to practice backing up. You need ten pennies. Arrange them like this:

You can move only three pennies. Make the arrangement point in the opposite direction.

One way to begin: Start moving pennies. That's the Plunge-Right-In method. Not bad. If it works.

But look at it backwards. You already know where you have to end up. What's the same about both arrangements? What's different?

(Hint: This drawing helps to show you which three to move.)

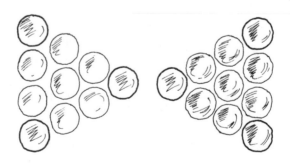

The Six Glasses Problem

A second practice. For this one you need six glasses, three empty and three with some water in them. Line them up like this:

You may touch and move only one glass. Change the line so no empty is next to another empty and no full is next to another full.

It may help to get six more glasses. (Don't start this one in the kitchen right before someone is starting to fix dinner.) Arrange them as they should be at the end of the problem. Can you see now which glass to move?

(Hint: No one said pouring was illegal. Watch out for those mental blinders.)

The answer to "Blowing Bits": Just hold four
while you blow one off. Then hold three.
Blow again. And on and on.

The Orange Juice and the Water Problem

While you're at the kitchen table, try this. You need just two glasses. They should be the same size and the same shape. They both should have the same amount in them. One has water in it. The other has orange juice. (You can use water with a bit of food coloring.)

Take a spoonful from the glass of orange juice and put it in the glass of water. Mix it up. Now take a spoonful from the glass of water (with the orange juice in it) and put it in the glass of orange juice. Mix it well.

Once again. Put a spoonful from the orange juice glass into the water glass. And then a spoonful from the water glass back into the orange juice glass.

Now for the problem. (No, that wasn't the problem. All that was just to get you ready.)

Is there more orange juice in the water glass than there is water in the orange juice glass? Or the same of each in each?

Really.

This one is complicated. But starting at the end is the only way.

The Checker Tournament

More practice for working backwards: At a checker tournament, there were sixty-four players. It was an elimination tournament. When a player lost, that player was out of the running. How many games were played before there was a champion?

Now wait a minute. Don't start dividing and adding. Start from the end. There is one winner. That makes how many losers? And each lost one game? Hmmmmm.

The Two Jugs

One more: Suppose you have two jugs. One holds five liters. One holds three. You need exactly four liters. How can you do it?

Don't start by pouring. That may get you going in a useless direction. Not to say anything about the water you'll waste.

Picture where you want to end up. Now try to back up to see how to get there.

Keep this backwards approach in mind when a problem strikes. Sometimes it makes a solution pop right out. Sometimes it gives you a fresh start when going forward just didn't work.

It's Smart to Ask

Sometimes you don't ask a question because it seems dumb. Like when you're sitting in class not really understanding what's going on. Everyone else seems to know. You don't feel right asking.

Sometimes someone else asks just what was on your mind. What a relief.

Successful problem solvers can't go around hoping someone else will ask the questions.

The answer to "Face to Face": Any doorway will do. Place the sheet of newspaper so half is on one side of the door and half is on the other, with the door closed in between.

Try this. Here are some real simple questions to ask people. They are about stuff everyone knows. Things so common, no one even bothers to ask about them. You'll learn it's not so dumb to ask what seems obvious. And you'll get some practice in asking.

Why do girls' shirts button one way and boys' shirts in the opposite way?
Why do most chairs have four legs?
Why do so many kids like to play baseball?
Why are most rooms either square or rectangular?

The idea here is not to get the answer. The idea is to get some practice asking questions. Try asking different people the same question. It's interesting to see how many different kinds of answers you'll get.

Asking questions is a good way to find out about something. Asking useful questions is even better. Here's an exercise to get you to sharpen up your questions.

You Only Get Three

This is an "imagine" exercise. You are a TV interviewer. On your program, different people come to be interviewed. You want to learn as much about each person as possible. You have time to ask only three questions. What three questions would you ask for each of these people?

A kid your age who has an identical twin.
A teacher who has just received the award for Teacher of the Year.
A person who has just won a million dollars in a contest.
A person who won a million dollars in a contest a year ago.
A famous athlete who was forced to stop playing because of a broken leg.

The answer to "Puzzling Ping-Pong": Fill the hole with water. The ball will float up.

Sometimes the most important person to ask questions of is yourself. Here are some push-ups to practice questioning. Each of these stories is like a riddle. But there is a reasonable explanation for each. To solve the problem, you need to ask yourself questions like these:

What don't you know about the situation?
What do you know about the situation?
What more do you need to know?

A Wet Story
A man went for a walk. It started to rain. He didn't have a hat. He wasn't carrying an umbrella. He kept walking. His clothes got wet. His shoes got wet. Still, his hair didn't get wet. How come?

A Dry Story
A woman unwrapped a lump of sugar. She put it into her coffee. The sugar did not get wet. How can this be?

Try these on other people. Tell them one of the stories. They may ask you any questions they want with one rule: You must be able to answer their questions with either a yes or a no. You can learn a lot from questions other people ask.

A Running Story

A man was running home. Near home he met a masked man. He stopped. Then he turned around and ran back to where he started. Why?

A Mysterious Story

Peter, Mary, Bill and Sally live in the same house. One night Peter and Mary went out to the movies. When they got back they found Sally beat up and dead on the floor. Bill was not arrested. He was not questioned for any crime. Why not?

Letting Your Mind Run Wild

There are times when thinking crazy on purpose is a good idea. Not acting crazy, thinking crazy. You can let your mind run wild in different ways. Try these running wild exercises.

Make a list. The topic is: What this world needs is . . . .

See how many possibilities you can think of.

Lots of things might have been invented just that way. Who ever thought there could be an oven that could boil water in a cup without the cup getting hot, that could bake a potato in four minutes? Who ever thought there could be a machine small enough to fit in your hand that could do all your arithmetic for you? Someone did. The ideas may have seemed crazy at one time. But they came true. How many things in science fiction stories have come true?

If you like to draw, try these. Draw a solution for each of these problems.

A machine that would automatically make your bed in the morning.
A machine that would help you go to sleep.
A peach picking machine.
A machine that would turn the pages of a book when you're reading in bed and your hands are cold.

Think about things in new and crazy ways. Here are some to get you started. For each question, make a choice. There are no right answers. Think about why you chose what you did.

Which is taller, red or brown?
Which is heavier, a stretch or a sack of apples?
Which takes up more space, a laugh or a television?
Which is funnier, g or q?

Here's something to do the next time someone taps you on your shoulder and says, "Guess what?" Surprise them. Guess. A really good guess.

Some push-ups. Letting your mind go wild may be the only way to tackle these.

What Comes Next?

Some easy ones first to give you the idea. What comes next in each of these?

A, B, C, D, E, ___ , ___ , ___ , . . .
A, B, A, C, A, D, A, ___ , ___ , ___ , . . .
A, D, G, J, M, ___ , ___ , ___ , . . .

Get the idea? Here come the crazies. The solutions are really very sensible answers.

O, T, T, F, F, ___ , ___ , ___ , . . .
M, T, W, T, ___ , ___ , ___ .
J, F, M, A, M, ___ , ___ , ___ , ___ , ___ , ___ , ___ .

(Hint: The first one can go on forever. The other two end when the spaces there are filled in.)

Crazy Toothpicking

You need to use toothpicks for each of these.

1. Use NINE toothpicks to make TEN.
2. Use SIX toothpicks to make ZERO.
3. Use toothpicks to show that SIX and FIVE make NINE.
4. Use toothpicks to show that half of ELEVEN is SIX.

Had enough for now? From time to time, practice letting your mind go. What doesn't seem to have anything to do with a problem may be just the thing. Take a chance. Try out what seems like a crazy idea. Maybe it won't work.

(But it's better than being bored sitting around with your head in your hands.)

The answer to "The Checker Tournament": Sixty-three games were played.

Have You Seen Something
Like This Before?

Another approach to problems is to find a problem like the one you've already got. It may be a problem you have already solved. It may be a problem that you could solve more easily. In either case, you'll get a boost for your thinking. A helpful clue. A push in the right direction.

In real life, very often the same problem crops up over and over. Sometimes it's disguised a bit. But if you don't learn from your first solution, you'll just keep getting the problem again. And again. That's no way to go through life.

First, here are two problems that are similar to others in this book. See if the solutions to those problems help you here.

The Paper Match Problem

If you drop a paper match, it will land flat on its side. What can you do so when you drop it, it will land balanced on an edge?

(Hint: A related problem is in "Don't Fall for What Pops In First.")

A Family Fact

Explain this: A boy's grandfather is only six years older than the boy's father.

(Hint: A related problem can be found in "Putting Your Foot In Your Brain.")

The answer to "A Mysterious Story": Bill was a cat. Sally was a fish.

Now, three more problems:

Does a Flying Canary Weigh?

Suppose you've got a large bottle with a canary inside. The bottle is sealed, and it's on a scale. The canary is standing on the bottom of the bottle. Then the canary starts to fly around inside of it. Does the reading on the scale change?

This can be complicated to think about. And probably not possible to test. No fair putting a canary in a closed bottle.

What you need is a related problem. Suppose the bottle were filled with water and a catfish were inside. Would the scale read differently when the fish was resting on the bottom or swimming around?

And for some real sticky problems to think about: What if the bottle were open instead of sealed? What if the canary were in a cage instead of in a bottle?

The answer to "The Orange Juice and the Water Problem": At the end of the problem, both the orange juice and water glasses have the same amounts of liquid in them as when they started. But they're mixed up a bit. The orange juice in the water glass replaced some of the water that used to be there. That much water is now in the orange juice glass. Both those amounts are the same.

The Ship in the Bottle Problem

Maybe you've seen them. Ships inside bottles. The neck of the bottle is real small. How did the ship get inside?

Here's some information that may be useful to you. It's possible to buy bottles with full-grown pears in them. The pear flavors what has been poured into the bottle — syrup, brandy, whatever. How do pears get inside? Like the ship's bottle, the neck is too small to squeeze a pear through. The way it's done is that the bottle is attached to the branch of a pear tree when the pear is very small. The pear grows up inside the bottle. The bottle is like a miniature greenhouse.

Okay, back to the ship. They don't grow like pears. But they have to be smaller to fit through the neck of the bottle.

The Bathroom Scale Problems

This time, you try to think of a related problem. Make your predictions. Then test them out.

What happens if you stand on a bathroom scale and lift one foot up? What will the scale read?

Suppose you have two bathroom scales. If you stand on both of them, one foot on each, what will they read? If you put one scale on top of the other, and then stand on the two of them, what will the scales read?

Suppose you took one scale into an elevator. What would happen if you stood on it while the elevator went up and down? Aside from the other people in the elevator looking at you funny.

Don't ignore what you already know. That might be the best first clue to tackling any new problem. Try to think of a problem that is similar. The new problem may not be so new after all.

The answer to "A Wet Story": The man was bald.

Getting Into Someone Else's Head

It's been said that two heads are better than one. Then maybe twenty heads are even better. For some problems, it helps to have other people's opinions. Then you can make up your mind from the choices. Or make an entirely new choice.

That's when taking a poll can be useful. It's a way of finding out how other people think. It's done a lot. As in TV ratings and newspaper columns.

Here's a problem to try a poll on. It's the fried egg problem.

The answer to "The Two Jugs": Fill the five-liter jug and pour as much of that as you can into the three-liter jug. Now empty the three liters. Then put the two left in the larger jug into the three-liter jug. Fill the five-liter jug again. Use it to fill the three-liter jug. There are already two liters in the three-liter jug, so it will take one more. Four are left in the five-liter jug.

Picture a fried egg, cooked so the white is all set and not at all goopy. The yolk is bright yellow, a cheerful bubble. And the whole thing is in the middle of the plate. Got all that? (If not, go back to the section on "Sharpening Your Senses.")

Here comes the problem: How can you eat the egg so that the yolk doesn't run all over the plate, but ends up inside you?

Here's what not to say about this problem:

Bleh. Runny yolks are yukky. Cook the egg until it's hard.
If that's the only way you like your fried eggs, wait a while.
When you grow up, different things taste good. Meanwhile
stick with the runny egg problem.

It's impossible. The yolk always gets all over the plate.
Nope. Remember, impossible isn't allowed in this book.

*There's only one way to do it. Mop it up with a piece of
bread.*
Nope again. One-way thinking will get you nowhere.

Here's what you might say about this problem:

Yeah, that is a problem.
I know one way, but I bet there are lots more.

Now you're thinking. Here's what you might do about this
problem: Take a poll.

There are other ways to eat the egg.

You could put the egg on a piece of bread and break the yolk so it runs on the white. The extra gets absorbed by the bread. Eat quickly.

You could cut off little pieces of the white and dip them in the yolk. You need to time it right. By the time you use up all the white, there shouldn't be any yolk left.

You could eat the white only. Soon all that's left is the yolk. Carefully slide your fork under the entire yolk. Be careful not to prick it. Pop the whole yolk into your mouth. Now, break it and let it slide down.

Start asking around. And start eating some more eggs. Test the different methods. This problem might even work into a public interest article for your school paper.

There are lots of problems where the more heads at work the better. Polls can help for these kinds of problems. Like how can you stop from chewing on your fingernails? Or how can you best ask your mom if you can spend the night at a friend's house so she'll say yes?

The answer to "A Running Story": It was a baseball game. The man was on third. The masked man was the catcher.

Other people aren't always handy when you need them. So another thing to do is to learn to think like another person. Or two. Or three.

That takes some practice. It means really thinking about how other people see the world. Kind of opening up your own thinking.

Try this exercise.

A girl's dog followed her to school.
It wasn't allowed in the school.
But it sat outside her room barking and whining.

The rest of the kids thought it was funny.
The teacher didn't.

The girl tried to get her dog to go home.
All it did was wag its tail and try to lick her face.

Finally the teacher told the girl she had to call home.
The school newspaper put this story in its next edition.

Imagine how you would tell this story if you were the girl. How about if you were the teacher? The dog? Or the newspaper reporter?

Imagine what it would be like for each of the characters. Ask a friend to try this and compare stories.

Try this exercise next time you're reading a story or watching a TV program. Try to feel what other people's lives are like. Next time you're feeling angry at someone in an argument, imagine why they're thinking the way they are. If you're brave, the two of you could stop the argument, switch so you each pretend you're the other, and continue the argument. Then you have to be the other person for a little bit. Maybe this can help you see why grownups seem to act strangely sometimes.

The answer to "A Dry Story": The woman put the sugar into a can of ground coffee.

The Path Game

Here's another way to practice getting into someone else's head. It's a game for two people that calls for solving a problem.

You need a sheet of paper and a pencil. And a blindfold if one of you absolutely can't manage to keep your eyes shut without peeking. One person is the tracer and isn't allowed to look.

The other follows these directions: Draw a path on the paper with the pencil. You may not lift the pencil until you're done. The path can go in any direction. It can cross itself. It can be easy or complicated. Put an arrow at the start and an X at the end. Give the blindfolded player the pencil and position it at your arrow.

The problem: You want the other player to trace over your path. You can give any directions you want. You may not touch the pencil or the person's hand.

It's important to play the game at least twice so you can try both parts. Here's what to look for:

How do the two paths compare? (Maybe you should use two different colored pencils.)
What snags did you run into?
Did the other person understand your directions?
Were the other person's directions the same as yours or different?
Can you think of a totally different way to give directions?

Think about what you can learn from all this. Besides finding other ways to approach problems, you'll see how different people think differently. The more clues you get about that, the more easily you can think differently when you need to. It's a handy skill.

The answers to "Crazy Toothpicking":

1. TEN   2. 0
3. NINE   4. X̶ǂ

The Pillow Method

There are some problems that totally stump you. You have no ideas. Not even wrong ones. One big blank.

What you need is some inspiration. A brand new angle. A little hope. *Something!*

At times like these, the best help might be your pillow. Sleep on it. Not just on the pillow, but on the problem, too. Let it roll around up there in your head.

You might be surprised. The answer might just appear at the strangest time.

Right now, you might be thinking: *That doesn't seem like a very good way to tackle a problem.*

There is the possibility that the pillow method won't help at all. There is no guaranteed way to solve problems. But you didn't seem to be doing much better on your own.

Some people have reported other uses of the pillow for solving problems. Like punching it. Or throwing it across the room. Who knows when that might spark the very idea you need.

The Bear Story

Have you heard the old problem about the bear? It walked one mile south. Then it turned and walked one mile east. Then it turned again and walked one mile north. It wound up right back where it started. What color was the bear?

Maybe you need to sleep on that one.

The answers to "What Comes Next?": Each letter is the first letter of the words in these sequences:
One, Two, Three, Four, Five, Six, Seven, . . .
Monday, Tuesday, Wednesday, Thursday, Friday, Saturday, Sunday.
January, February, March, April, May, June, July, August, . . .

How Do You Know When You're Really Right?

This book is only practice. The problems in it are not your problems. They're to help you get ready for the real thing. That's what you bump into at home, at school, outside.

Out in the world, problems usually don't sit around by themselves. They seem to be tied up with lots of other things. Many times there are no clear solutions. There may be several possible answers, not just one.

It's not easy to know when you're right. Thinking about thinking can help you get a head start.

The End

P.S. The bear was white.